Bannockburn School Dist. 106
2165 Telegraph Road
Bannockburn, Illinois 60015

DATE DUE

Science Alive

Energy

Chris Oxlade & Terry Jennings

A+

Smart Apple Media

Smart Apple Media is published by Black Rabbit Books
P.O. Box 3263, Mankato, Minnesota 56002

Printed in China

Created by Q2A Media
Series Editor: Honor Head
Book Editor: Katie Dicker
Senior Art Designers: Ashita Murgai, Nishant Mudgal
Designer: Harleen Mehta
Picture Researcher: Poloumi Ghosh
Line Artists: Indernil Ganguly, Rishi Bhardhwaj
Illustrators: Kusum Kala, Sanyogita Lal

Library of Congress Cataloging-in-Publication Data

Oxlade, Chris.
    Energy / Chris Oxlade and Terry Jennings.
    p. cm.—(Smart Apple Media. Science alive)
    Summary: "Explains essential facts about energy, including the difference between kinetic and potential energy,
different energy sources, and how energy changes and is transferred. Includes experiments"—Provided by publisher.
    Includes index.
    ISBN 978-1-59920-273-0
    1. Force and energy—Juvenile literature. 2. Power resources—Juvenile literature. I. Jennings, Terry J. II. Title.
QC73.4.O938 2009
531'.6—dc22
                                                                                                2007049121

All words in **bold** can be found in "Words to Remember" on pages 30–31.

Web site information is correct at time of going to press. However, the publishers cannot
accept liability for any information or links found on third-party web sites.

Picture credits
t=top b=bottom c=center l=left r=right m=middle
Cover Images: Main Image: Berry Dean/Index Stock Imagery/Photolibrary   Small Image: Fred Goldstein/Shutterstock:
Nikolay Titov/ Shutterstock: 4r, Emin Kuliyev/ Shutterstock: 5, rpbirdman/ istockphoto: 6b, Edward Parker / Alamy: 8l,
Coleman Outrider: 9b, Tom Stewart/ Corbis: 12, FredS/ Shutterstock: 13tr, Peter Arnold, Inc. / Alamy: 14b, A. T. Willett
/ Alamy: 15tr, Anouchka/ istockphoto: 18b, Kapoor Baldev/ Sygma/Corbis: 19b, Harris Shiffman/ Shutterstock: 20b,
IRC/ Shutterstock: 25tl, Uko_jesita/ Dreamstime: 25br, Johner/ GettyImages: 28b, Sapsiwai/ Dreamstime: 29bl, Jozsef
Szasz-Fabian/ Shutterstock: 29bl, Kcc008/ Dreamstime:29bl, Vincent Giordano/ Shutterstock: 29bl.

9 8 7 6 5 4 3 2 1

Contents

What Is Energy? 4

Forms of Energy 6

Energy Changes 8

Try This... Stored Energy 10

Heat Energy 12

Losing Energy 14

Try This... Convection Currents 16

Energy Sources 18

Making Electricity 20

Try This... Generating Electricity 22

Renewable Energy 24

Try This... Catching Radiation 26

Energy for Life 28

Words to Remember 30

Index 32

Web Finder 32

What Is Energy?

Energy is very important in our daily lives. We cannot see or touch energy, but it causes all the changes that we see around us.

Energy for Life

The food we eat gives us the energy we need to move around and to grow. We need energy to play and to work. We even need energy when we are asleep.

▶ *Energy is helping this boy to kick the ball.*

Types of Energy

Light, sound, heat, and electricity are all types of energy. We use huge amounts of energy in our homes, stores, schools, and factories.

◀ In this city, energy is used to provide heat, light, and power for the buildings. Energy also makes the cars and buses run.

Forms of Energy

Different types of energy can be seen all around us. Anything that moves has energy. Some energy can be stored before it is used.

Movement Energy

Falling objects and flying birds have energy because they are moving. The heavier an object is, and the faster it moves, the more movement energy it has. Movement energy is also called kinetic energy.

▲ *This flying eagle has movement energy. When it quickly swoops down to pick up its prey, it has even more energy.*

Stored Energy

A stretched rubber band is a form of stored energy. This energy is released as movement energy when you let go of the band.

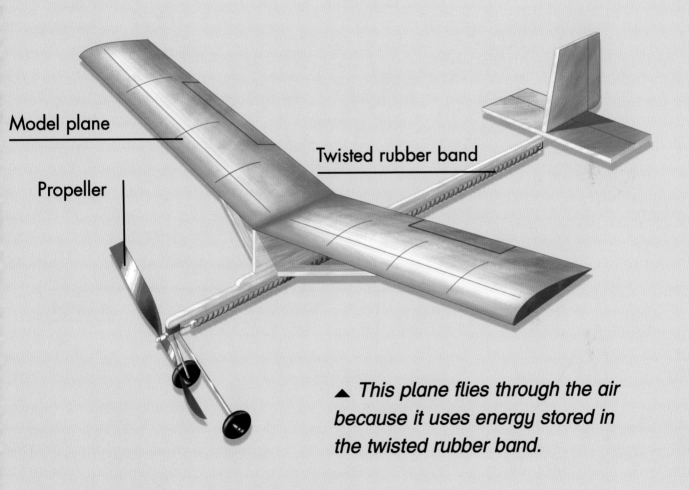

Model plane

Propeller

Twisted rubber band

▲ *This plane flies through the air because it uses energy stored in the twisted rubber band.*

Fuels

Fuels such as coal, oil, and gas have energy stored in them, too. The energy is released as heat and light when the fuel is burned. Stored energy is sometimes called potential energy.

Energy Changes

Although we can change one type of energy into another, we cannot make energy from nothing. Energy cannot be made or destroyed.

Sound Energy

When an object moves, it causes **vibrations** in the air. These vibrations move through the air as sound waves. When they reach your ears, you hear the waves as a sound.

◀ *This boy is changing movement energy into sound energy when he beats the drum.*

Movement Energy

When a ball is thrown straight up in the air, it has movement energy. However, as the ball rises, it slows down and the energy changes to stored energy. This stored energy changes back to movement energy again when the ball begins to fall.

▶ *The ball rises and stops before it falls.*

Changing Electricity

Electrical energy can be changed into lots of other types of energy. An electric heater turns electricity into heat, a light bulb changes electricity into light, and an electric motor turns electricity into movement.

Handle

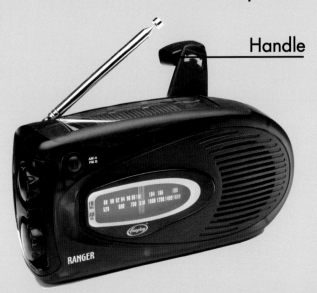

◀ *Turning the handle of this wind-up radio changes movement energy into electricity. The electricity then changes to sound energy.*

9

Try This...
Stored Energy

Discover how a rubber band stores energy and then releases it.

You Will Need

- a small rubber band • a wooden thread spool
- a thumb tack • a small birthday candle

1 Push the rubber band through the hole in the thread spool. Attach one end of the rubber band to the end of the thread spool by pushing a thumb tack through its loop and into the spool.

2 Slide the candle through the rubber band at the other end of the spool. Wind the candle around until the rubber band is twisted.

3 Put the spool on a table and let go.

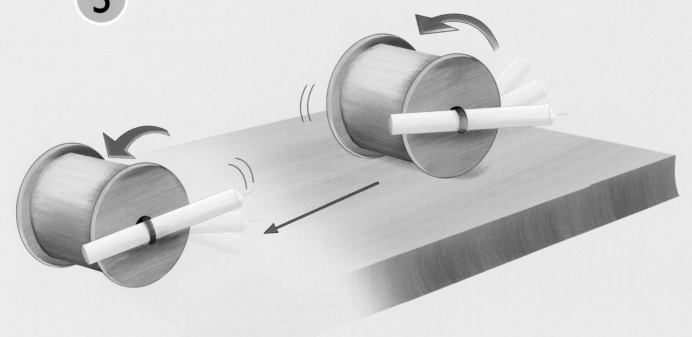

What happened?

The rubber band will slowly unwind, pushing the spool along. During this experiment, you have used chemical energy in your body (that works your muscles) to twist the band. This energy is stored in the rubber band. The stored energy is then turned into movement energy when you let go of the candle and the spool.

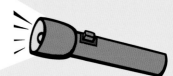

Heat Energy

For thousands of years, people have used fire for heat energy and light energy. We still use heat energy to cook our food, to keep us warm, and to give us hot water.

▲ *A fire is a good way to keep warm when you are camping. It can also be used to cook food. But fire is dangerous, and we must use it with care!*

Heat and Temperature

Temperature is a measurement of how hot or cold an object is. Hot objects have more energy than cold objects. We use a thermometer to measure how hot or cold something is.

▶ *The liquid in this thermometer expands and moves up when the temperature of the air rises.*

Moving Heat

Heat energy always moves from hotter objects to colder objects. If you leave a metal spoon in a hot drink, the handle of the spoon quickly becomes hot. This is called **conduction.** Heat can spread through gases and liquids, too. This process is called **convection.**

▶ *When you heat water in a pan, the water at the bottom becomes hot first. The warm water expands and rises. The cooler water then takes its place.*

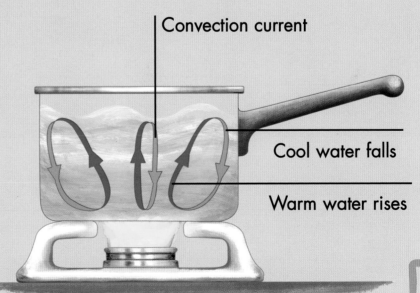

Convection current

Cool water falls

Warm water rises

Losing Energy

In cold weather, the heat energy we use to warm our homes seems to disappear. Where does the energy go?

Escaping Heat

Most of the energy we lose goes into the air. When we heat our homes, the heat gradually escapes through the roof, walls, doors, and windows, and it warms the air outside.

▲ *This special photograph shows that heat energy is escaping from the windows (the white areas) of this warm house in winter.*

Insulation

Some materials do not let heat pass through them very easily. These materials are called **insulators.** One of the best insulators is air. Many of the clothes and other materials we use to keep warm have air trapped inside them.

▶ *This man is putting insulation in a building to stop heat from escaping through the walls and the roof. The tiny fibers in the material have lots of air trapped between them.*

Friction

Energy can also be lost because of a force called **friction,** when touching surfaces try to slide past each other. When we rub our hands together, for example, they get warm. This is because friction has changed movement energy into heat energy.

Try This...
Convection Currents

Look at how heat travels in water.

You Will Need
- a large jar • a heat-proof bowl • an eye-dropper
- food coloring

1 Fill the jar with cold water. Leave the jar standing still for a few minutes for the water to become still.

2 Ask an adult to help you pour some hot (not boiling) water into the bowl.

3 Carefully stand the jar in the bowl and wait a few minutes. Use the eye-dropper to put some food coloring into the water in the jar and watch how it moves.

What happened?

You should see that the food coloring moves around the jar. This shows the movement of convection currents in the jar. The water at the bottom rises to the top when it becomes warm. This water is replaced by colder water, which warms up, too.

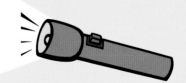

Energy Sources

The energy we use for lighting, heating, cooking, and for running machines comes from many different sources.

Fossil Fuels

Coal, oil, and gas are the most common energy sources. We use these **fossil fuels** for heating and cooking and for producing electricity.

◀ We get energy from fossil fuels by burning them. The burning gas from this stove releases heat and light energy.

Wood Energy

In some countries, families cook their meals over a wood fire. This is because other fuels are not available or are too expensive. Wood is a popular fuel, but we need to keep growing trees so there is enough wood for us to use.

Environmental Problems

When fuels burn, they release carbon dioxide gas. It is believed that high levels of carbon dioxide are causing the Earth's temperatures to rise. We call this problem **global warming.**

▲ *Global warming is causing the ice around the North and South Poles to melt. Floods like this will become more common if sea levels rise.*

Making Electricity

Electricity is a very useful form of energy. It can be changed into heat, light, sound, and movement energy.

Power Plants

Most of the electricity we use is produced at a power plant. Most power plants burn fossil fuels to boil water to make steam. This steam is used to power a machine called a **generator** to make electricity.

▲ *Inside these generators, a huge magnet turns inside a coil of copper wire. This turns movement energy into electricity.*

Powering Our Homes

The electricity produced at a power plant reaches our homes through a series of wires that travel both above ground and underground.

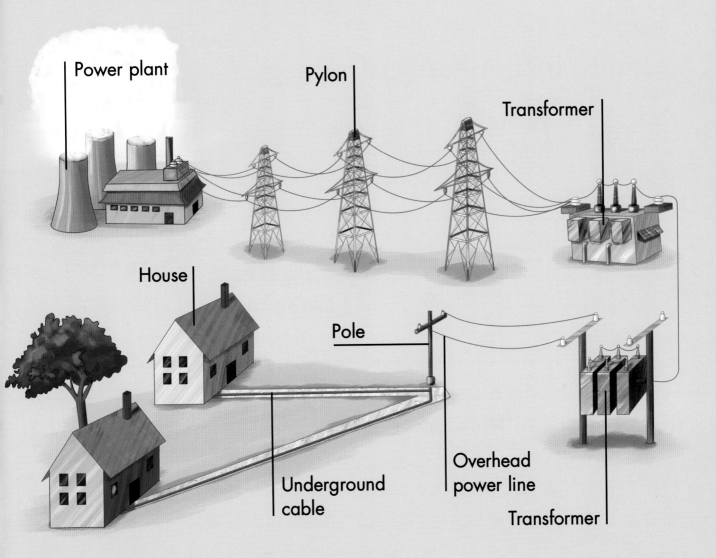

Power plant

Pylon

Transformer

House

Pole

Underground cable

Overhead power line

Transformer

Portable Electricity

A **battery** can be used to power small devices, such as flashlights and radios, with electricity. A battery is full of chemicals that produce electricity. Once the chemicals are used up, the battery runs out. However, some batteries can be **recharged.**

Try This...
Generating Electricity

Look at how movement energy can be turned into electrical energy.

You Will Need
• 6.5 feet (2 m) of connecting wire • a compass • a bar magnet

1 Ask an adult to help you to strip about 3/4 inch (2 cm) of insulation from each end of the wire.

2 Starting about 4 inches (10 cm) from one end of the wire, make about 15 turns around the center of the compass.

3 Halfway along the remaining wire, make 10 turns of wire loosely around your thumb. Lift the coil off your thumb carefully.

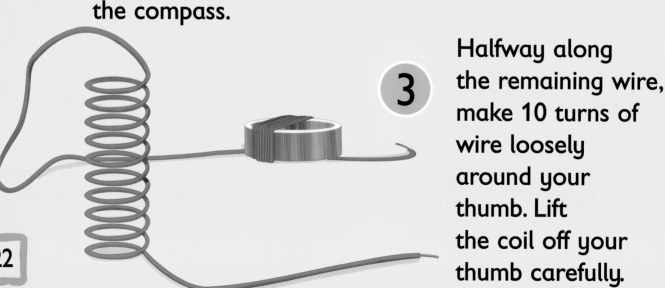

4 Wind the two ends of wire together to complete a loop. Stand a bar magnet on a table and carefully put the coil over the magnet. Move it down and up quickly while you watch the compass needle.

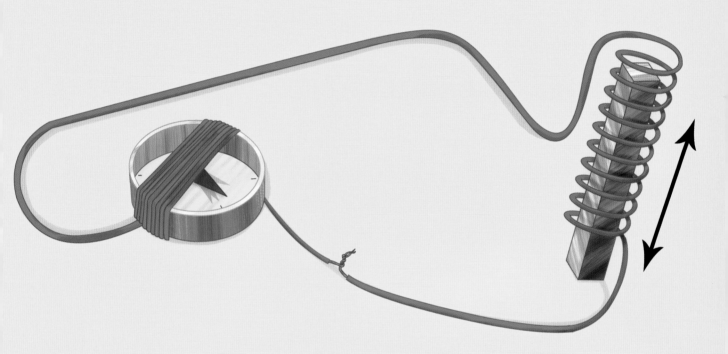

What happened?

The needle should twitch when you move the coil up or down over the magnet. This shows that electricity is flowing through the wire. Some of the movement energy from your hand is turned into electrical energy in the coil. This is because the coil moves through a magnetic field.

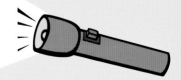

Renewable Energy

Some energy comes from the wind, the sun, flowing water, and ocean tides. These **renewable** sources of energy can be used again and again.

Energy from Water

At a **hydroelectric** power plant, river water is stored behind a large wall, called a dam. The water is then released so that it flows through **turbines.** The turbines power generators that produce electricity.

▲ *Water flows down to the base of this dam. It powers generators to produce electricity.*

Turbine

Wind Energy

When the wind blows, the air has movement energy. We can use this energy to produce electricity. A wind turbine has large blades that are turned by the wind. Each turbine spins a generator.

◀ *A wind farm with hundreds of turbines produces the same amount of electricity as a small coal-fired power plant.*

Energy from the Sun

Solar energy is heat and light energy from the sun. Solar panels can be used to trap the sun's heat. This heat can be used to make hot water for radiators or for washing.

Solar panels

▶ *The solar panels on this roof use* **solar cells** *to turn sunlight into energy for the home.*

Try This...
Catching Radiation

Find out how a solar panel captures heat radiation from the sun.

You Will Need

• white paper • black paper • 2 small cardboard boxes (the same size), without lids • tape or glue • plastic wrap • 2 thermometers

1 Cut sheets of white paper to cover the inside surfaces of one of the boxes. Tape or glue them in place. Do the same with black paper.

2 Ask an adult to help you pierce a hole in the side of each box for a thermometer to fit through. Cover the top of each box with plastic wrap.

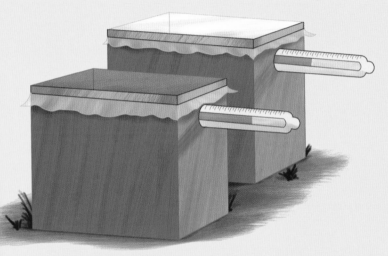

3 Put both boxes outside on a sunny day. Position them so that the sun's rays go straight into the boxes. After a few minutes, use the thermometers to measure the temperature inside each box.

What happened?

The air temperature should be warmer in the black box and cooler in the white box. Black surfaces absorb heat well. The black surface has heated the air inside the box, making it warmer. White surfaces reflect heat. This is why the air in the white box is cooler.

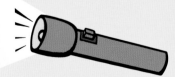

Energy for Life

All living things need energy. Plants use energy from the sun to make their **food**. Animals get their energy by eating plants or other animals that have eaten plants.

Food Energy

Food gives us energy to move and to keep warm. Energy from food also keeps parts of our body in good working order. The energy from food keeps us alive.

▲ *All living plants get the energy they need from the sun.*

Plant Energy

Green plants contain a chemical called chlorophyll, which gives them their green color. Chlorophyll uses the energy from sunlight to make food. This process is called **photosynthesis.** Water and carbon dioxide are used and oxygen is released.

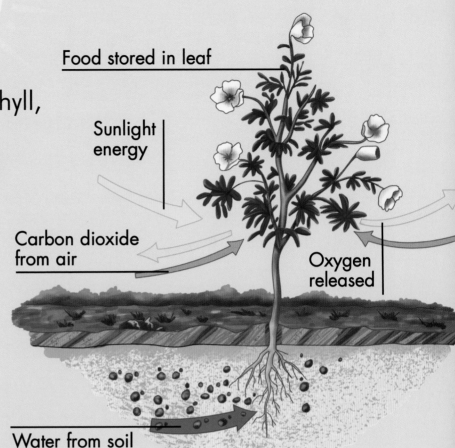

Food stored in leaf

Sunlight energy

Carbon dioxide from air

Oxygen released

Water from soil

Energy Foods

Different foods contain different amounts of energy. Food packaging tells you how much energy each food contains. Eating a variety of foods is the best way to keep healthy.

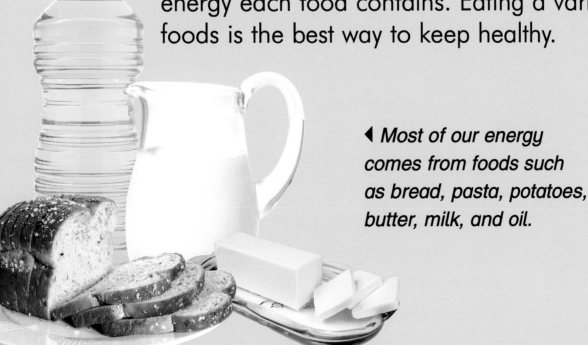

◀ *Most of our energy comes from foods such as bread, pasta, potatoes, butter, milk, and oil.*

Words to Remember

Battery
A container of chemicals that can produce electricity.

Conduction
When heat passes through a material easily.

Convection
When gases or liquids move from a cooler area to a warmer area.

Food
Food provides energy for living things to grow.

Fossil fuel
A fuel formed from the remains of ancient plants and animals.

Friction
A force that slows down two surfaces sliding past each other.

Fuels
Materials that release energy when burned.

Generator
A machine that produces electricity.

Global warming
The warming of Earth's atmosphere.

Hydroelectric
Using the energy of running water to generate electricity.

Insulators
Materials that do not allow heat to pass through.

Photosynthesis
The process by which plants make their food.

Recharge
To store energy in a battery's chemicals so it can be reused.

Renewable
Something that will not run out.

Solar cells
Devices used to change sunlight into electricity.

Temperature
A measure of hotness or coldness.

Turbines
Large fans turned by steam, wind, or water.

Vibrations
Quick movements (from side to side, up and down, or back and forth).

Index

conduction 13

convection 13,
   16–17

energy sources
   18–20, 24–25,
   28–29

energy types
   chemical 11, 21
   electrical 5, 9,
      18, 20–21,
      22–23, 24
   food 4, 28, 29
   heat 5, 7, 9,
      12–15, 18, 20,
      25, 26, 27

energy types
   (continued)
   light 5, 7, 9,
      12, 18, 20
   movement 6–7,
      8–9, 11, 15,
      20, 22–23, 25
   renewable 24–25
   sound 5, 8, 9, 20
   stored 6, 7, 9,
      10–11

friction 15
fuels 7, 18–20

global warming 19

insulation 15

photosynthesis 29
power plant 20,
   21, 24, 25

sun 24–27, 28, 29

temperature 13, 27

water 20, 24, 29
wind 24, 25

Web Finder

For Kids:

http://www.eia.doe.gov/kids/

http://www.kids.esdb.bg/

http://tiki.oneworld.net/energy/energy.html

http://www.energyquest.ca.gov/index.html

For Teachers:

http://www.teach-nology.com/teachers/lesson_plans/science/
   physics/electricity/

http://www1.eere.energy.gov/education/lesson_plans.html

http://www.energy.gov/foreducators.htm